POP CLASSICS FOR TWO

2	Africa
4	Alone
6	Can't Smile Without You
8	Centerfold
10	Dancing Queen
12	Dust in the Wind
14	Every Breath You Take
16	Eye of the Tiger
18	I Melt with You
20	I Still Haven't Found What I'm Looking For
22	Imagine
24	Jessie's Girl
26	Lean on Me
28	Piano Man
30	Right Here Waiting
32	Silly Love Songs
34	The Sound of Silence
36	Stand by Me
38	Sweet Caroline
40	Take on Me
42	Time After Time
44	We Built This City
46	You Are So Beautiful

Arrangements by Mark Phillips

ISBN 978-1-5400-6536-0

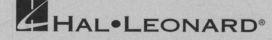

HAL•LEONARD®

Visit Hal Leonard Online at
www.halleonard.com

Contact us:
Hal Leonard
7777 West Bluemound Road
Milwaukee, WI 53213
Email: info@halleonard.com

In Europe, contact:
Hal Leonard Europe Limited
42 Wigmore Street
Marylebone, London, W1U 2RN
Email: info@halleonardeurope.com

In Australia, contact:
Hal Leonard Australia Pty. Ltd.
4 Lentara Court
Cheltenham, Victoria, 3192 Australia
Email: info@halleonard.com.au

AFRICA

TRUMPETS

Words and Music by DAVID PAICH
and JEFF PORCARO

Play 3 times

To Coda ⊕

2nd time, D.S. al Coda
(take repeats)

CODA ⊕

ALONE

TRUMPETS

Words and Music by BILLY STEINBERG
and TOM KELLY

CAN'T SMILE WITHOUT YOU

TRUMPETS

Words and Music by CHRIS ARNOLD,
DAVID MARTIN and GEOFF MORROW

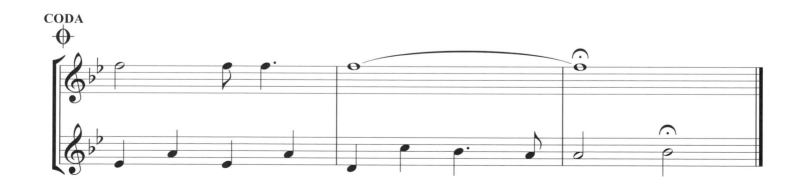

CENTERFOLD

TRUMPETS

Words and Music by
SETH JUSTMAN

DANCING QUEEN

TRUMPETS

Words and Music by BENNY ANDERSSON,
BJÖRN ULVAEUS and STIG ANDERSON

DUST IN THE WIND

TRUMPETS

Words and Music by
KERRY LIVGREN

EVERY BREATH YOU TAKE

TRUMPETS

Words and Music by
STING

EYE OF THE TIGER

Theme from ROCKY III

TRUMPETS

Words and Music by FRANK SULLIVAN
and JIM PETERIK

I MELT WITH YOU

TRUMPETS

Words and Music by RICHARD IAN BROWN,
MICHAEL FRANCIS CONROY, ROBERT JAMES GREY,
GARY FRANCES McDOWELL and STEPHEN JAMES WALKER

I STILL HAVEN'T FOUND WHAT I'M LOOKING FOR

TRUMPETS

Words and Music by
U2

IMAGINE

TRUMPETS

Words and Music by
JOHN LENNON

JESSIE'S GIRL

TRUMPETS

Words and Music by
RICK SPRINGFIELD

LEAN ON ME

TRUMPETS

Words and Music by
BILL WITHERS

PIANO MAN

TRUMPETS

Words and Music by
BILLY JOEL

RIGHT HERE WAITING

TRUMPETS

Words and Music by
RICHARD MARX

SILLY LOVE SONGS

TRUMPETS

Words and Music by PAUL McCARTNEY
and LINDA McCARTNEY

THE SOUND OF SILENCE

TRUMPETS

Words and Music by
PAUL SIMON

STAND BY ME

TRUMPETS

Words and Music by JERRY LEIBER,
MIKE STOLLER and BEN E. KING

SWEET CAROLINE

TRUMPETS

Words and Music by
NEIL DIAMOND

CODA

2nd time, D.C. al Coda

TAKE ON ME

TRUMPETS

Words by PAL WAAKTAAR
and MAGNE FURUHOLMNE
Words by PAL WAAKTAAR,
MAGNE FURUHOLMNE and MORTN HARKET

(small notes optional)

TIME AFTER TIME

TRUMPETS

Words and Music by CYNDI LAUPER
and ROB HYMAN

WE BUILT THIS CITY

TRUMPETS

Words and Music by BERNIE TAUPIN,
MARTIN PAGE, DENNIS LAMBERT
and PETER WOLF

YOU ARE SO BEAUTIFUL

TRUMPETS

Words and Music by BILLY PRESTON
and BRUCE FISHER